$16.95 Aust School Supplies

967.62

$16.95 Aust School Supplies

Fleur Ng'weno

FOCUS ON
KENYA

Evans Brothers Limited

Published by Evans Brothers Limited
2A Portman Mansions
Chiltern Street
London W1M 1LE

First published in Great Britain in 1990 by
Hamish Hamilton Children's Books

© Fleur Ng'weno 1990

Reprinted 1993, 1994

Design by Andrew Shoolbred
Map by Tony Garrett

1 Kenya – Desc & tr
Series

Printed in Hong Kong by Dah Hua Printing Co. Ltd.

ISBN 0 237 60194 X

The author and publishers would like to thank
Camerapix for permission to reproduce all the
photographs in this book.

Cover Traditional baskets, now made of sisal fibres, are
popular all over the world. Craftswomen make them in
a variety of colours and patterns to keep up with the
changing fashions.

Title page At a waterhole in the sand, a girl fills water
containers: tall leather pots, rounded gourds, which are the
fruits of plants, and split gourds called calabashes.

Opposite An open-air market. The bananas will be cooked
while they are still green and hard. Umbrellas
protect the market traders from strong sun and sudden
rain.

Contents

Introducing Kenya

Kenya is a country on the eastern coast of Africa, right on the equator. It is a land of striking landscapes, ranging from snow-capped Mount Kenya to rich farmlands, barren deserts and tropical beaches. Early people – our ancestors – lived there more than a million years ago, scientists say. Today, Kenya is a meeting place of many cultures. It is also famous for its wildlife, which includes the greatest assortment of large mammals left anywhere on Earth.

Kenya is a fairly large country, the size of France. Its population is small, but growing rapidly. Most Kenyans are country people – small-scale, independent farmers and ranchers. Only about 25% of the people live in urban areas, one of the lowest percentages in the world. Kenya's capital, Nairobi, is a modern city near the centre of the country.

People

The people of Kenya usually have dark brown skin and tightly curled hair, like most Africans. But they vary a lot in height, build and features, and speak many different languages. Over the years, people from Europe, Asia and Arabia have settled in Kenya too, bringing their own languages and customs. The official languages in Kenya are English and Swahili.

Connections

For thousands of years, ships have sailed to the coast of Kenya from Arabia and southern Asia. Today, telecommunications and airlines link Kenya with the rest of the world. A network of roads and railway lines connects Kenya with its neighbours Tanzania, Uganda, Sudan, Ethiopia and Somalia. The countries of eastern Africa, however, are separated from North Africa by the Sahara Desert, and from West Africa by the forests of Zaire. There are roads and trains to the south, and trade with the countries of southern Africa is increasing.

Landforms and seasons

Ancient rocks form the backbone of Africa, including the western part of Kenya. The Rift Valley, a great gash in the Earth's crust, cuts across the country. East of the Rift, the central highlands slope down to grassy plains, dry thornbush country, and the ocean.

There are two types of season in Kenya, wet and dry. Rains are important, because water is often scarce in Kenya. The absence or presence of water is a major influence on the lives of the people. Most people live in the south and west, where there is enough rainfall.

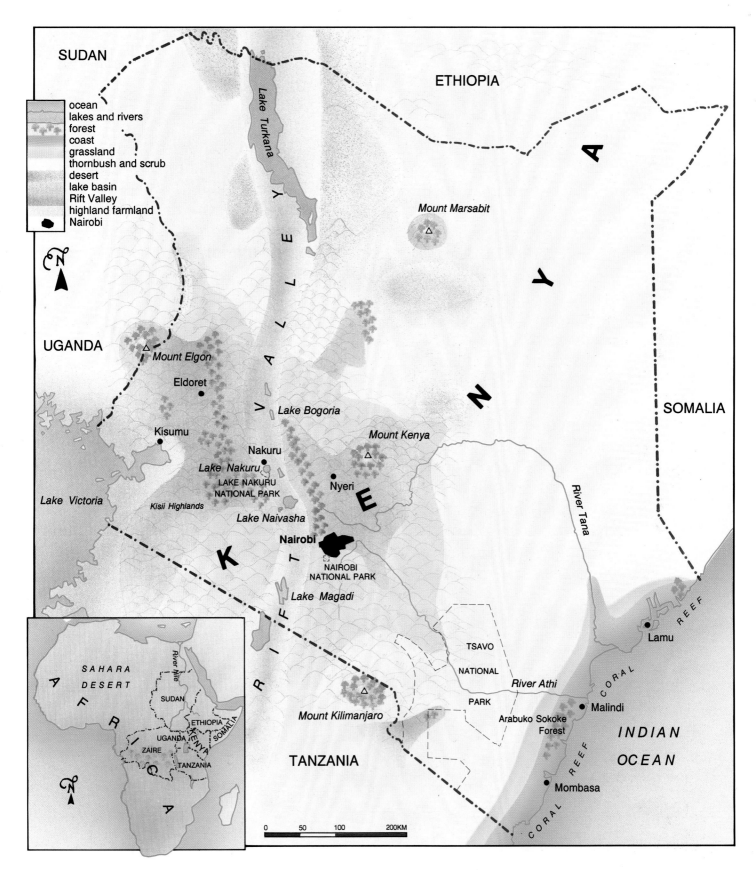

SUDAN

ETHIOPIA

ocean
lakes and rivers
forest
coast
grassland
thornbush and scrub
desert
lake basin
Rift Valley
highland farmland
Nairobi

N

Lake Turkana

Mount Marsabit

UGANDA

Mount Elgon

Eldoret

Lake Bogoria

SOMALIA

Mount Kenya

Kisumu

Nakuru

Lake Nakuru

LAKE NAKURU
NATIONAL PARK

Nyeri

Lake Victoria

Kisii Highlands

Lake Naivasha

Nairobi

River Tana

NAIROBI
NATIONAL PARK

Lake Magadi

TSAVO

Lamu

NATIONAL

River Athi

REEF

PARK

Malindi

Mount Kilimanjaro

Arabuko Sokoke
Forest

INDIAN

OCEAN

TANZANIA

Mombasa

*SAHARA
DESERT*

River Nile

*A
F
R
I
C
A*

SUDAN

ETHIOPIA

UGANDA

KENYA

SOMALIA

ZAIRE

TANZANIA

N

0   50   100   200KM

The coast

The fringing reef

The waves of the Indian Ocean crash on coral reefs along the whole length of the Kenya coast. The reefs are broken only where fresh water enters the sea. A coral reef is formed by tiny animals called coral polyps. They take minerals from seawater to build stony cups around themselves. These cups, massed together, form the coral reef. Millions and millions of coral polyps, working over hundreds and thousands of years, help to build the reef.

The reef is a stony mass, breaking the force of the waves. Its surface is dotted with tunnels and overhangs, nooks and crannies. It is the habitat for countless living things: starfish and shells, prawns and crabs, algae and sea anemones. Brightly coloured fish, with vivid dots and stripes, swim among the coral 'gardens'.

To explore this undersea world, a person just puts on a glass mask, and swims or wades among the coral gardens which make up the reef. Several national parks and reserves in Kenya are located underwater!

The edge of the sea

Sandy beaches, cliffs of old coral, and mangrove forests line the shore. Mangrove trees grow in mud and salty water where land meets sea. Poles from mangroves are strong and resistant to rot, and used to be a traditional export from the coast.

Fishermen use mangrove poles to push their dug-out canoes through shallow water. They lay fish traps made of basketwork, with a funnel-shaped entrance. Fish find it easy to go in but hard to get out, and so they are trapped.

◄ On the coral reef, sea anemones use their stinging tentacles to catch small fish. The orange clownfish is not harmed by the anemone's sting. It lives in safety among the tentacles and helps to attract other fish for the anemone to eat.

► Coconut trees have endless uses, including thatching for the roof.

The climate on the coast is hot and humid. Malaria occurs there, as in other lowland, tropical areas. Malaria is a disease that is carried by some mosquitoes. People who get malaria may become very ill and even die, but they are usually cured by medicine. Malaria can be prevented by taking anti-malarial tablets regularly.

The sacred groves

Once a great forest grew inland from the sea. Its mighty trees were holy groves to the people and sheltered large herds of elephants. Now only patches of the forest remain. Some rare animals and plants, including a kind of African violet, are found only in the coastal forest.

Tourist hotels and plantations of coconut, cashew nut, sisal and sugar cane now line the coast road. The sparkling beaches, cooled by sea breezes, are important tourist attractions. Along the roadside, market places are shaded by large mango trees. The low, square houses are made of white-and-brown coral rock. Their roofs are thatched with coconut fronds.

Swahili

Swahili is a language in the Bantu language group of Africa. It is spoken by the people living on the coast of East Africa. Swahili was written in Arabic script for hundreds of years. Today, it is usually written in Roman letters, like English, French and Spanish. Traditional Swahili poetry, with its special rhythm, is an important form of literature on the Kenya coast.

Swahili words often heard

Jambo!	Hello! (Answer: Jambo!)
Harambee!	Let us pull together! Now refers to self-help community projects or fund-raising events.
Nyayo!	Footprints; now refers to following leaders in peace and unity and with care for others.
Uhuru	Freedom; also, independence.
Mwananchi	Man or woman of the land; ordinary person, citizen. Plural: Wananchi.
Mheshimiwa	Honourable; respectful way to address someone
Mzee	Elder, old man; friendly way to address a man
Mama	Mother; respectful way to address a woman
Mtoto	Child. Plural: Watoto
Safari	Journey
Mpira	Football
Shamba	Farm or garden
Asante	Thank you
Kwaheri	Good-bye

Coconut seller reading a Swahili newspaper.

Coastal life

The people who first lived in the coastal forest were hunters and farmers. They built houses of woven poles, covered in grass thatch and protected by strong wooden fences. They prayed in their traditional religion. Celebrations included dances to the sound of drums, flutes, xylophones, rattles and other instruments.

Centuries ago, traders from Arabia came to Kenya in sailing ships called *dhows*. They anchored in the natural harbours of Lamu, Malindi and Mombasa. They set up trading businesses and married people of the coast. They built Arab towns with houses of several storeys, narrow streets, and mosques so they could worship in their religion, Islam.

Going 'up-country'

People from Britain and northern Europe arrived in Mombasa in the late nineteenth century. At first, the people were mainly Christian missionaries and traders. They built churches for Christian worship and houses in the European style.

The British wanted to travel and trade inland. They decided to build a railway line from Mombasa to reach Uganda, near Lake Victoria. People from India came to work on the railway line. They too settled in Kenya, taking up jobs as shopkeepers, clerks and skilled workers.

Nowadays, *dhows* still sail from Arabian countries to the Kenyan coast, as they have done for thousands of years.

▲ Fort Jesus was built by Portuguese explorers in the 16th century. It is now a museum.

◄ At the oil refinery near Mombasa, imported petroleum is refined into petrol and other products for Kenya and neighbouring countries.

Mombasa

Mombasa is an island, separated from the mainland by a sheltered, deep-water harbour. The port of Mombasa is a major African seaport, handling cargo for Kenya and its land-locked neighbours. Two of Kenya's biggest industries, an oil refinery and a portland cement factory, are located near the port.

People from all over Kenya now work at the ports, in the factories and in the beach hotels. Many coastal people continue their traditional occupations, as farmers, fishermen, craftsmen, traders and Islamic scholars.

The pace of life in Mombasa is suited to the hot climate. Shops are open in the morning, then close for a long break during the heat of day. In the warm evenings, the streets are busy with people shopping, strolling and eating outdoors. Coastal cooking is rich and varied, with a lot of fish and rice and many dishes cooked in coconut milk.

Shops in Mombasa, and most other Kenyan towns, are usually small. Some sell only *khangas* – rectangular pieces of cloth in bright colours and designs. Many women wear khangas, wrapped around their waists and shoulders. Muslim women often wear the black, loose-fitting *bui-bui* dress, with a black head covering. On the coast, many people are Muslim, and the festivals and ceremonies of Islam are an important part of their lives.

The grasslands

Between the snowy peaks of Africa's highest mountains, Mount Kenya and Kilimanjaro, and in many parts of Kenya, there are grasslands. Scattered trees and bushes may grow in the grassland, which is sometimes called a savannah. This is the habitat for East Africa's great herds of large mammals.

The changing seasons

In the long dry season, the grasslands turn yellow or grey. Trees and bushes shed their leaves. Little dust storms rise like puffs of smoke from the dry ground. Animals gather from near and far to drink at river pools and waterholes. Fires sweep through the dry grass, charring the ground. Then at last the sky darkens with clouds, and the rains break.

Rain touches the land like magic. Overnight, trees put out new leaves and plants begin to grow. Where fires blazed, wild flowers now bloom, and the blackened ground turns bright green with young grass. Water collects in hollows, forming pools. Frogs, toads and insects arrive to mate and lay their eggs. During the rainy season, rainstorms alternate with sunshine, and the grass grows.

The game-filled plain

To avoid competition, different plant-eating animals eat different kinds of food.

Elephant herds are made up of family groups of females and young, led by the old females.

In this way, there is enough food for all. Long-necked giraffes browse on the leaves of trees. Most antelopes feed on tender grass and leafy plants, while zebras can chew tough dry grass. Hippopotamus rest in cool rivers during the day, then walk out to graze on sedge and grass at night. Rhinoceros browse on the twigs and leaves of bushes. Elephants feed on a variety of plant material, from leaves and grasses to fruits, roots and tree bark. They sometimes bring down trees to get at the tender bark or leafy branches.

Feeding on the great plant-eating herds are a smaller number of meat-eating predators. Lions hunt in family groups called prides, stalking carefully to surprise their prey. Hyenas are both hunters and scavengers, usually hunting in packs. A leopard often drops on its prey from a tree, while a cheetah runs down its prey with a brilliant burst of speed. The dog-like jackals eat scraps from the kills of other animals, and also hunt insects and rodents.

Birds

Flocks of cattle egrets follow the mammal herds to catch the insects disturbed by their feet. Oxpeckers, or tickbirds, ride on the mammals' backs and eat the ticks right off the skin. Ostriches often feed among the mammals. Ostriches are the biggest birds in the world. They do not fly, but can run very fast. Vultures eat dead animals, and help keep the grasslands clean.

Insects

A variety of insects have important roles to play in the food chains and webs of the grasslands. Ticks and biting flies hatch with the rains and feed on mammal blood. Dung beetles roll mammal dung into balls. They lay their eggs on the dung balls and bury them, so their young will have plenty to eat when they hatch out.

Termites also feed on dung as well as dry grass, fallen branches, dead trees and wooden houses. Termite mounds rise like towers all over the grasslands; some are up to three metres high.

The oxpecker on the giraffe's neck is feeding on the ticks that feed on the giraffe.

Inside a termite mound is a network of tunnels and chambers. In some chambers, termites make compost heaps from the dead plant material they collect. The termites eat the fungi which grow on the compost heaps. And when adult termites fly from their mounds to mate, they become food for birds and small animals.

11

Cattle-keepers

The people who live in the grasslands have traditionally kept animals. The land is usually too dry to grow cultivated crops. The livestock they keep are suited to the climate. African sheep have short, red-brown wool. The cattle have a big flap of skin on the neck, which helps them to sweat and stay cool in hot weather.

Cattle and culture

Cattle are very important to the people of the grasslands and provide the staple food, milk. Milk is very nourishing, lacking only iron and some vitamins. People get iron from the meat of sheep and goats, or by cooking blood taken from one of their cattle. Wild fruits provide vitamins. Religious and social ceremonies often include the giving or slaughtering of cattle.

Cattle provide for basic needs but, in return, the people must be ready to move when their cattle need water or fresh pasture. Cattle usually have to drink every day.

The people build temporary houses, surrounded by a fence of thornbushes, since they will have to move again. The houses are made of mud mixed with cow dung, over a frame of poles; the dung helps to keep the walls smooth and waterproof. When they move, the people carry everything with them – clothing, household goods, jewellery and keepsakes.

Pastoral, or herding, people live in close-knit communities. Each person belongs to an age-set of people born in the same few years. People of the same age-set take part in the stages of life ceremonies together. Young women of one age-set marry at about the same time. Young men go off to become warriors, and herd the cattle in the dry season.

In the dry season, pastoralists move their herds in search of water and green pasture.

Young warriors playing *mbao*, a traditional board game. This board is cut into the ground.

In some places, wheat fields have replaced grasslands.

From nomads to ranchers

The traditional way of life in the grasslands is changing little by little. Kenya has imported foreign breeds of cattle. These cattle produce more meat or milk, but have less resistance to tick-borne diseases. People build cattle dips to wash the cattle with chemicals that kill ticks. When there are many ticks, the cattle must be dipped every week. People want to stay near the cattle dips, so they may settle in one place, and become ranchers.

Families also stay in one place in order to send their children to school. If their parents are always moving, children have to go to boarding schools. Many families have settled on farms, and are growing crops suited to dry land. Some grasslands are now large-scale wheat farms, and in places, the wheat fields grow right down to national park boundaries.

New ways of life

The national parks and a growing tourist industry have created new jobs in the grasslands. People work in the parks as game rangers and gatekeepers, in hotels and tented camps, and as tour guides and drivers. Others set up shops selling snacks, carvings of animals, or beautiful beaded jewellery to the tourists.

Jewellery is a work of art that can be carried from place to place when the community moves.

13

Green highlands

The highlands around Mount Kenya in central Kenya, and Mount Elgon in the west, provide ideal growing conditions for many different plants. The deep soil, red-brown to almost purple in colour, is well-watered and fertile. A variety of crops thrive in the cool temperatures and year-round sunshine of the high altitudes.

Mount Kenya towers above the mountain forests.

Forested slopes

On the highest mountains, wild flowers bloom among clumps of grass in the open moorlands. Below the moorlands, there are great trees, covered with mosses, lichens and ferns. A belt of bamboo forest circles the high mountain slopes. The bamboo grows so thick and tall that an elephant disappears instantly among the rustling stalks. Forests of native cedar, olive and *podocarpus* trees clothe the lower slopes. Black and white colobus monkeys blend into the pale lichens that hang from dark branches.

Below the natural mountain forests there are plantations of pine and cypress trees. They provide softwood for timber and paper-making. A paper factory in western Kenya makes paper for both local use and export. In this part of Kenya, some houses are made of wood. Elsewhere, there are very few houses made of wood, because timber is often scarce, and termites will eat wooden structures.

Water power

In the cool mountain air, water vapour condenses to form clouds and falls as rain. Moorland grasses, forests and bamboo filter the rain as it falls to the ground. Clear streams rise from springs and rush down the mountain slopes.

A tea plantation. Tea bushes come from China but Kenya is said to produce the finest tea leaves.

Each red coffee berry contains two seeds or 'beans'. Arabica coffee bushes are native to eastern Africa.

There are few rivers in Kenya, and they are not very big. But because they drop so steeply from the mountains to the sea, they can be used to produce electricity. Several small hydroelectric dams have been built along the River Tana, flowing east from Mount Kenya. These dams produce more than half of Kenya's electricity.

Farm country

Small mixed farms, a few hectares or less in size, cover most of the highlands. The farmer's family live on the farm, not in the village, and eat the food they grow. Some farms are on steep slopes, but the clay soil sticks together and there is little erosion. In drier areas, farms are larger, with rolling fields of barley or herds of cattle and white woolly sheep. Some big commercial farms have immense plantations of tea, coffee or pineapples.

Trading centres

Many roads have been built to help highland farmers send their produce to markets or factories. Trading centres and small towns have grown along the roadsides and railway lines, and some have become important commercial centres.

Eldoret in the western highlands is Kenya's boom town. Among its industries are cotton, wool and synthetic textile mills, as well as factories processing agricultural produce such as mushrooms, milk products, cereals and tannin.

> **IRIO: a recipe from the highlands**
> Put whole potatoes, maize kernels and green peas in a heavy cooking pot or covered saucepan. Add water to cover, and bring to boil. Reduce heat and simmer until tender.
> Add some 'greens' such as spinach or pumpkin leaves, and salt to taste. Cook for ten minutes, then mash the food together. Serve hot, plain, with butter, or with a meat stew.

Highland farmers

Farming people in the highlands have to work hard. Mornings are often bitterly cold. The cattle have to be milked, and some of the milk is taken to the roadside to be collected by the dairy. Children usually fetch water from a stream, spring or tap some distance away. The small family farms are scattered all over the countryside, so most children have a long walk to school, sometimes more than five kilometres. Many children walk all the way home for a hot lunch, and then all the way back to school.

A small highland farm

A hedge or fence usually borders the small farm. The houses and sheds are round or square, with roofs of thatch or iron sheets.

Farm animals include dairy cows, a few goats, sheep or donkeys, a flock of chickens and a guard dog.

The land is divided into small neat plots. Cash crops, such as coffee, are sold for export. Food crops, such as maize and potatoes, are grown for the family or sold locally. A clump of banana trees is usually planted near the house, and a few scraggly eucalyptus trees provide firewood. Many small farmers have market gardens, producing vegetables for sale in the towns.

Sun-up to sundown

Farm work includes planting, weeding, harvesting and plucking tea leaves or coffee berries. Most farm work is done by hand. Only large farms normally have tractors.

A group of small farms in the highlands. Vets and agricultural extension officers often visit farmers to discuss their problems and suggest solutions.

Boys herding dairy cattle. The mountain in the background is Mount Kenya.

Pyrethrum in the field looks like silvery-leaved daisies. The flowers are dried and powdered to make a natural insecticide, safer to use than chemical insecticides.

The midday sun is hot, but it quickly gets cold in the evening. Children who take livestock out to graze wear thick jumpers and may carry a tin with burning charcoal to warm themselves.

Maize and millet

Maize, or corn, is the staple food at mealtimes. It is usually ground into flour, or cornmeal, then boiled and stirred until it is a solid mass. The ground meal used to be made from millet, a traditional African crop. White maize, native to the Americas, has now replaced millet in most homes.

The cooked maizemeal, generally called *ugali*, is served with stews of meat or vegetables or cooked as porridge for breakfast. Maize is also boiled with beans, or mashed with potatoes and vegetables.

Food for a highland family comes from a variety of plants, with a little meat and milk. This is quite different from the diet of a pastoral family in the grasslands. Their food is mostly milk and meat, with a few fruits or vegetables.

Woman shelling maize with her children. The maize cobs are stored in the granary behind them.

Land of milk and honey

Half of Kenya is the arid north – long stretches of grey or orange sand, distant horizons, shimmering heat, thorny trees, and in some places, no plants at all. The dry season may last for a whole year. In the brief rainy season, the land turns emerald green, deserts become lakes, and roads are impassable.

Strange as it may seem, this harsh, hot, dry land really is a land of milk and honey. These are the basic foods here. The people herd camels, and sometimes cattle, sheep, goats and donkeys. Camels' milk is their daily food. Honey hunters gather honey made from flower nectar by wild bees to use as food and drink.

The wide-open spaces — house in northern Kenya.

The nomadic life

During the dry season, rivers disappear into the sand and plants stop growing. The camel herds browse on bushes. Camels can go for a week or two without water, but sooner or later they must drink. People dig deep wells to find water for their families and livestock. Thousands of camels may gather at large waterholes.

When a whole settlement has to move, the people pack up all their belongings, including the houses! A house is a framework of bent poles, covered with panels of thatch and sheets of leather. The poles, coverings, household goods, milk gourds, water pots, pets and children are loaded onto a camel, ready to go.

Livestock is wealth, and sometimes the young men go on raids to steal animals from their neighbours. The Kenya police

Everything the family owns must be portable.

Mounted policemen on camels chase cattle rustlers.

have a special anti-stock-theft unit to catch cattle thieves. The policemen use horses and camels instead of vehicles.

The wide-open spaces

In most of northern and eastern Kenya there are few people, few towns and few roads. Light aircraft are widely used for transport in this vast land. Doctors and nurses fly in for monthly clinics. National Park wardens spot poachers from the air. The light aircraft airport in Nairobi is one of the busiest in the world.

The people of northern and north-eastern Kenya come from several different ethnic groups. They may be Muslims or Christians, or they may follow traditional religions. Some of their ancestors travelled down from north-eastern Africa, and many customs and traditions recall the customs of ancient Israel and Arabia.

Acacia trees are hardy plants that can survive drought, fire and flood. Most acacias have long, sharp thorns, protecting them from browsing animals. Flat-topped, wide-spreading acacias provide shade in open country. Their fallen seed-pods are food for livestock and wild animals, and their wood is used as firewood and for making tools.

Lake Victoria

The great lake

Lake Victoria is shared by Kenya, Uganda and Tanzania. It is the world's second largest freshwater lake and the main source of the River Nile. Its shores are edged with papyrus reeds, tall narrow stems topped by a bunch of stalks with tiny flowers.

Fishermen go out on the lake in wooden boats painted in bright colours and designs. Among their catch are tilapia and Nile perch. Tilapia fish are medium-sized and are eaten fresh or smoked. Nile perch become huge, up to two metres long. They make excellent eating, and are shipped, frozen, for sale in Nairobi and Mombasa.

Dramatic thunderstorms often build up over the lake. The Kisii highlands in south-western Kenya probably get more thunderstorms than any other place on Earth – thunder on 250 days a year!

Country life

The green hills and flat lowlands near the lake are the most densely settled rural areas of Kenya. There is enough rain here to grow a variety of crops. Most of the people live on small farms, growing crops and raising animals for their daily needs.

Many homesteads are built in traditional style. Each house consists of a round framework of poles, carefully plastered with mud, with openings for doors and windows. The outside walls are often decorated in earth colours. The pointed, thatched roof keeps the house cool and airy in the hot weather.

A fisherman sets his traps near a clump of papyrus reeds on the shores of Lake Victoria.

A potter adds the finishing touches to her clay pots.

There are usually several houses in the compound, each one is a room for the parents, the boys or the girls. In some families, a man marries a second wife; then each wife has her own house. Grain stores are built near the houses. They look like small houses on stilts.

Farm animals are brought into an enclosure at night. In the lowlands, euphorbia bushes are planted as hedges around the whole compound. Euphorbia bushes have green stems and branches but no leaves; their milky juice is poisonous.

Farmers grow millet, maize, cassava and bananas as basic foods. Different millets are cooked like rice or maizemeal for dinner, or as porridge for breakfast. Some millets are brewed into beer. Cooking bananas, a special variety, are picked when they are green and hard, then steamed or boiled. Cassava is a root crop that survives long dry periods in the ground. It can be eaten like potatoes or ground into flour.

It is tiring to work the land in the hot climate. Many people also suffer from bilharzia (schistosomiasis), a disease caused by tiny parasites. The parasites spend part of their life in freshwater snails. People catch bilharzia when they wade in water, such as lake edges and irrigation ditches, where infected snails live. Bilharzia makes a person feel very tired and weak. It can be treated with medicines, but many people just catch it again.

A blend of cultures

The town of Kisumu is Kenya's main lake port. There are many churches, mosques and schools in this heavily populated area. Most of the people are Christians, belonging to several different churches. The people wear western clothes for everyday use, but for dances and ceremonies they have wonderful costumes: robes of animal skins, masks from woven fibres and head-dresses of tusks, horns and shells. They play many musical instruments: bells, rattles, horns and an eight-stringed harp.

Dancing and singing are important in ceremonies.

21

The Great Rift Valley

The road going west from Nairobi winds up and down hills, climbing steadily. Suddenly, the land seems to fall away to the valley 300 metres below. Across the valley, 50 kilometres away, the western side of the Rift stands like a wall. The flat valley floor, with old volcanoes rising from it, stretches to the northern and southern horizons.

The lakes

A series of lakes are set like jewels on the valley floor. The largest is Lake Turkana, in the north-west. Its shallow, slightly

The Rift Valley is a section of the Earth's crust that is pulling apart very, very slowly.

Lake Nakuru is famous for its millions of flamingoes. The birds use the fringes on their beaks to filter tiny plants called algae from the water.

alkaline waters are full of fish. Crocodiles and waterbirds nest on islands that were once volcanoes. Around the lake, most of the land is low, barren and windswept. Few plants grow there, and the people live by herding, fishing and tourism. The volcanic soil of the Rift Valley is very fertile, but it is productive only where there is enough rainfall or irrigation.

Hot springs, steam jets and geysers bubble up from the ground in parts of the Rift Valley. They are formed when rainwater seeps down to hot volcanic rocks. Under heat and pressure, the water boils, expands and rises, spurting from the ground as steam or hot water. Foaming geysers bubble and roar on the shores of Lake Bogoria, a calm lake at the foot of the steep valley wall. Near Lake Naivasha, underground steam is tapped to generate electricity.

Minerals and mining

Lake Magadi, in southern Kenya, looks like vanilla, strawberry and pistachio ice cream. The lake is almost solid trona.

Trona is a mineral that is processed into washing soda, baking soda, salt and soda ash. The soda-rich water wells up from the ground in hot brine springs. Trona is snow-white, but bacteria in the water colour it pink or green in places.

Soda ash is Kenya's main mineral export. It is used in chemical, glass and soap industries. To mine and ship it, the Magadi Soda Company built a factory, a town, a road and a railway line. Lake Magadi lies in a hot, dry part of the Rift, a long drive from the city. Fresh water for the town is piped in from the valley wall and the school has a big swimming pool.

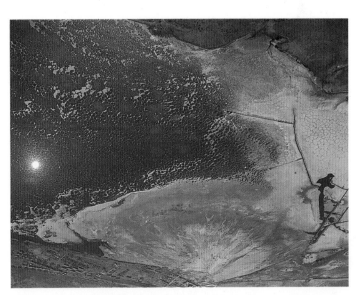
The mineral-rich waters of Lake Magadi.

Minerals and gemstones
Kenya's other mineral resources are mainly outside the Rift. Fluorspar, also called fluorite, is used in cement and steel manufacture and to make fluorine gas. Limestone is the major ingredient in cement, and marble makes handsome floors and walls. Gemstones from Kenya include red and green garnets, sapphires, rubies and Tsavorite.

Nairobi

Nairobi, 'the place of sweet waters', was built where rolling grasslands met forested hills, along the railway line. About 1½ million people live and work in the city. Most of them have come from the rural areas, and many of them return to the rural areas during holidays and after they retire.

The commercial centre

Nairobi is a city, a province, and the capital of Kenya. The National Assembly, the Law Courts, the Office of the President and the City Hall are in the centre of the city. About one hundred countries have embassies, high commissions or trade offices in Nairobi.

Nairobi is an international business and tourist centre, and people of many cultures live and work there. English is spoken all over the city, and some businesses advertise in French, German, Italian and Japanese. People can worship in Christian churches, Muslim mosques or Hindu temples. Restaurants serve almost every kind of food, from Korean dishes to fish and chips. Curries from India and Pakistan are very popular.

City shops include supermarkets, small shops and market stalls. Modern shopping malls are going up in the suburbs. In markets, curio shops or roadside stalls, shoppers usually bargain, or argue, over the price.

Nairobi began as a stop on the railway line.

City workers queue for piping-hot fast food snacks.

Nairobi streets are full of traffic.

Roads are filled with cars, buses, lorries, and a few bicycles, handcarts and wheelchairs. *Matatus* are passenger vehicles the size of small buses or large cars. They carry passengers in towns and all over the country. Kenyan drivers seem to think the crowded city is still the wide-open spaces and drive with careless speed. A pedestrian on the road is at risk, even on the zebra crossings.

The road from the airport passes between Nairobi National Park and the industrial area. The park is fenced on the city side, but wild animals wander freely in and out of the other side by crossing the River Athi.

In Nairobi, and elsewhere in Kenya, most factories are small, making items such as vehicle tyres, beer, chocolates, textiles and plastic products. There are also self-employed craftsmen who work by the side of the road. They hammer scrap metal into boxes, buckets, or charcoal-burning stoves. The informal sector provides jobs for many people, in small workshops, roadside stalls and cafés, and as street hawkers.

In and out of the city

Residential areas sprawl for many kilometres on all sides of Nairobi. Houses range from handsome mansions set in large gardens to crowded rows of maisonettes, four-storey blocks of flats, and shacks made of boxes and plastic sheets.

Black rhinoceros in Nairobi National Park.

History, politics and education

Years ago, most people in Kenya lived in small communities, and belonged to groups called clans. A council of elders made decisions for the community. People of different clans who spoke the same language and had the same customs were a tribe.

Land was usually owned by a clan or tribe, not by individuals. Families cleared plots for crops or brought herds to graze, then left the land to recover and become wild again.

Clash of cultures

European missionaries, traders and officials who arrived in Kenya did not understand this land use. They thought that if the land was not worked, it was not owned. So European settlers cleared the bush and hunted the wildlife. They cut the trees to fuel the railway, and brought in crops and livestock from Europe and the Americas.

British people settled in Kenya, and set up a local government. They were surprised when Africans complained, because they thought they brought development to Kenya. Africans saw that the best land was taken away from them. They had to work long and hard for low wages. Black people were treated harshly, and could not go to the same schools or social places as white people. These conditions eventually led to civil war.

From civil war to co-operation

From 1952 to 1957, there was a bitter civil war between the British settler government and African freedom fighters, often called the 'Mau Mau'. Many people were killed and suffered on both sides. After the war ended, talks began. Britain agreed that

The first president of Kenya, Jomo Kenyatta, consults with the second president, Daniel arap Moi.

Kenya would become independent on 12 December 1963, with an African government. British settlers could stay, but some had to sell their farms.

Independent Kenya has citizens of African, European, Asian and Arab ancestry. The country is governed by a president and a national assembly, or parliament, of 200 members. Local councils and District Development Committees make decisions at the local level. The first president of Kenya was Jomo Kenyatta, and the second, Daniel arap Moi.

Schools and jobs

Half the population of Kenya is under 15 years of age, and every child can go to primary school. That means a lot of schools, a lot of teachers, a lot of desks, books, papers, pens and chalk! The government spends more than a third of its budget on education, and parents help out

Many Kenyan students specialize in computer studies.

Schoolchildren singing a traditional song.

by building classrooms. All children wear school uniforms.

A big problem in Kenya is that there are so many young people who want a good education and a good job. There are not enough secondary school or university places for them all, or enough jobs in Kenya's young economy.

Many people are unemployed. Others are underemployed; they can only get seasonal, part-time or unskilled jobs. Some people turn to crime. There are jobs on farms and in rural schools, but many educated young people think they should get a desk job in town. The government is bringing piped water, telephones and electricity to the rural areas, to make them more attractive places in which to live.

Cultural traditions and pastimes

The average young Kenyan in the city wears the same blue jeans, listens to the same rock music, watches the same news on television and eats the same ice-cream as an average young Briton or American. Scholars must make an effort to keep African cultural traditions alive.

Stories

Story-tellers told stories to entertain, to teach and to record the history of the clan. Scary stories about ghosts and monsters helped to make children behave. Some tales explained why things are as they are.

The Hen and the Hawk

The hen and the hawk once lived together as friends. They shared each other's worldly goods and raised their children together.

The hawk had a very fine and sharp needle that she liked very much. Whenever the hen borrowed the needle, the hawk asked her to return it. The hen always promised she would. But one day the hen lost the needle in the garden.

When the hawk heard that her needle was lost, she became very angry. 'You promised to return it!' she cried.

'I'll find it, I'll find it,' said the hen, but the hawk was so angry that she swore to take revenge on the hen's children. The hen and her chicks ran away.

To this day, the hen scratches the ground, looking for the hawk's lost needle; and the chicks run away and hide whenever they see the hawk in the sky.

Popular folk tales in Kenya, and in much of Africa, include stories about Hare the trickster.

Music

Malaika, a Kenyan folk song in Swahili, became a world-wide hit. Today, choirs are a popular form of Kenyan music. The choirs blend church music and traditional songs with soloist and chorus. Songs are often composed for the occasion, such as praise for an event or a visiting official.

A flute player from the coast.

The fruits of gourd plants are dried and cleaned out inside so they can be used as containers.

Arts

Much of Kenyan art is in crafts. Everyday objects, such as stools or milk gourds, are beautifully decorated. Cowrie shells from the coast were traded far inland, to be used as money and ornaments.

Carved wooden animals and batik cloth, sold on street corners, are recent art forms. The sale of ivory was banned in Kenya in 1977 to protect elephants, and bangles and rings are now made of cowhorn.

Sports

Soccer is Kenya's favourite sport. Almost every school has a football pitch, and thousands watch the weekend league games. The Safari motor rally, held during the Easter holidays, also draws big crowds.

Drivers and their vehicles are pitted against mud, dust, rutted roads, steep slopes, rising rivers, and high-speed international rules.

It is Kenya's long-distance runners and boxers, however, who have reached the very top. Since the stylish Kipchoge Keino took the lead in 1964, Kenyan runners have never looked back. Kenyans have won the 3,000m steeplechase race in every Olympic Games they have entered from 1968 to 1992. In 1988, Robert Wangila became the first African to take Olympic gold in boxing.

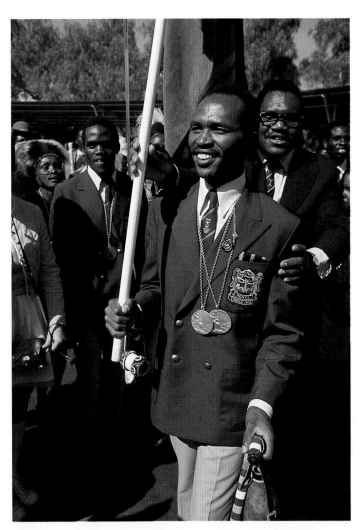

Kipchoge Keino, Kenya's first world record holder.

29

Kenya and the world

Human beings probably first walked on the Earth in the Rift Valley of eastern Africa, scientists say. Digging through the dry ground near Lake Turkana, they found the bones and tools of early humans. These first people lived on the lake shores more than a million and a half years ago. Richard Leakey, a famous Kenyan anthropologist, thinks they then travelled out of Africa to all parts of the world.

Slaves and students

During the days of the slave trade, many people were shipped from Kenya as slaves. Most of them went to Arabia. They became part of the population and did not make separate communities.

Today, thousands of Kenyans study in foreign countries, especially the United Kingdom, United States and India. They may work there for a short time, but most Kenyans sooner or later return to Kenya to help build the nation.

Famous people

Since independence in 1963, several Kenyans have made a mark on the world. Professor Thomas Odhiambo set up the International Centre for Insect Physiology and Ecology, where scientists study the lives and communication systems of insects. Michael Werikhe walks and talks to raise

Michael Werikhe, who walked across Europe in aid of the rhinoceros, meets an orphaned rhino calf.

money to protect the Black Rhinoceros. He has walked in East Africa and the United States. Khadija Adam's beautiful face graced the covers of fashion magazines as an international model, and K.K. Karanja was the chess champion of his age group in the United States at the age of twelve.

An international centre

More industrialised than most other East African countries, Kenya sells manufactured goods to its neighbours. Many companies and international organisations have their East African, African or world headquarters in Nairobi. Kenya is a member of the United Nations, the British Commonwealth, the Organisation of African Unity and the Preferential Trade Agreement for Eastern and Southern Africa.

The United Nations was formed by the countries of the world at the end of the

In the Kisii highlands near Lake Victoria, craftspeople carve animals, utensils, abstract images and even chess sets from the soft Kisii stone.

Second World War. Most nations belong to the UN, where they have a chance to discuss their problems instead of going to war. The United Nations also has agencies that specialise in certain subjects, such as health or trade, to help the people of the world. Almost all of the UN agencies have their headquarters in Europe or North America.

Two UN agencies are, however, based in Nairobi. They are the United Nations Environment Programme or UNEP for short, and Habitat, the United Nations Centre for Human Settlements. UNEP's activities include keeping track of threats to the world environment, such as pollution. One of Habitat's goals is to develop cheap, easy-to-build housing. Many international conferences are held in Nairobi. With its natural beauty and up-to-date facilities, Kenya is becoming an international centre for the environment.

The Kenyatta International Conference Centre is a landmark on the Nairobi city skyline.

Index and summary

Area:	582,650 square kilometres (225,000 square miles)
Population:	24 million (1992 estimate)
Ethnic groups:	*Coast:* Mijikenda (including Giriama and Digo), Swahili, Bajun, Pokomo, Arab.
	Grassland: Maasai, Samburu, Pokot.
	Highlands: Kikuyu, Kalenjin (including Nandi), Kipsigis and Tugen), Kamba, Embu, Meru, Taita.
	Northern Kenya: Oromo, Boran, Turkana, Rendille, Somali, Gabra.
	Western Kenya: Luliya (including Maragoli and Bukusu), Luo, Gusii, Kuria.
	Nairobi: Many African tribes, European, Asian (including Indian, Pakistani, Goan)
Main towns:	Nairobi, Mombasa, Kisumu, Nakuru, Eldoret, Nyeri
Highest point:	Mount Kenya, 5,199 metres
Longest river:	River Tana
Main agricultural produce:	Maize, beef and dairy products, wheat, sugar cane, beans, potatoes, millet, rice, tea, coffee, cotton, sisal
Main exports:	Coffee, tea, refined petroleum products, horticultural produce (fruits, flowers and fresh vegetables), meat and hides, pyrethrum
Main imports:	Machinery, industrial supplies and chemicals, vehicles and aircraft, petroleum, fertilizer
Official language:	English and Swahili
Currency:	Kenya shilling, divided into 100 cents
National airline:	Kenya Airways
Main newspapers and magazines:	Daily Nation, Standard, Kenya Times (dailies); Weekly Review (weekly); Rainbow (monthly, for children)
Radio and television:	KBC in English and Swahili, and KTN TV in Nairobi